PASSIVE INCOME

TOP 10 WAYS TO MAKE MONEY ONLINE

By

JEFF S. THOMSON

Table of Contents

Table of Contents

Legal Notes

Chapter 1. **Passive Income**

Chapter 2. **Blogging**

Chapter 3. **Photography**

Chapter 4. **Affiliate Marketing**

Chapter 5. **Sell Products On The Website**

Chapter 6. **Buy A Website**

Chapter 7. **Build An App**

Chapter 8. **Develop A Online Course**

Chapter 9. **Write An EBook**

Chapter 10. **Sell Your Own Products On The Internet**

Chapter 11. **Youtube**

LEGAL NOTES

Copyright © 2018 by Jeff Thomson.

All Right Reserved.

No part of this publication may be reproduced, distributed, or transmitted in any form or by any means, including photocopying, recording, or other electronic or mechanical methods, or by any information storage and retrieval system without the prior written permission of the publisher, except in the case of very brief quotations embodied in critical reviews and certain other noncommercial uses permitted by copyright law.

Chapter 1. Passive Income

What is Passive Income?

Are you searching for a proven, step-by-step system which allows you to make passive income streams automatically - with hardly any experience? Are you ready to begin making passive income, but have no idea where to start?

The idea of passive income is simple. You do some work once and generate income for years passively. Passive income is present, and thousands of people already are making money passively!

They aren't ways to turn your time into money directly. Instead, they are methods to plant seeds which means that your money shall grow, when you're sleeping or at the park walking your dog even. In other words, even when you're not out trying to create money actively.

It's all about the idea of passive income. As being a farmer who vegetation a crop tends the harvests and fields the produce, you can plant monetary seeds which will produce income.

It takes some ongoing build up front and some maintenance on the way, but in the event that you plant passive income seeds that match your climate you may bring in a nice harvest.

Passive income differs from attained portfolio and income in many ways. Passive income is thought as a stream of income gained with little effort generally, and it is known as progressive passive income when there is usually little effort needed from the average person receiving the passive income to be able to grow the blast of income.

Making passive income isn't unrealistic. But it isn't easy either. It takes effort and time to build a business that will later make you money regularly without spending a lot of time in front of your personal computer.

But the significant problem is that most people are not ready to take their business compared to that level plus they quit fast.

Earn thousands of dollars every month with these proven ideas. Discover what you should know about generating income online and achieving financial freedom with these top 10 income generating strategies and ideas.

With that said listed below are 10 legit methods for you to invest either time or cash today and receives a payment over and over again later on.

1. BLOGGING
2. PHOTOGRAPHY
3. AFFILIATE MARKETING
4. SELL PRODUCTS ON A WEBSITE
5. BUY A WEBSITE
6. BUILD AN APP
7. CREATE AN ONLINE COURSE
8. WRITE AN EBOOK
9. SELL YOUR OWN PRODUCTS ON THE INTERNET
10. YOUTUBE

Okay, Let's Start,

CHAPTER 2. **BLOGGING**

It's no real surprise that you would like to begin a blog. Blogging remains a marketing method that costs hardly any to create and peoples from all walks of life have created earning money blogs.

The problem about writing blogs is that it's actually not that difficult to do. When you can discuss something with knowledge, you can write a post.

Let talks about ways to take up a blog of yours.

Pick a Blogging Platform

There is a certain free blogging system like Blogger, which really is a publishing application from Google. With that said, this choice doesn't give your own blog domain name and hosting, which is important if you would like to be seen as professional and genuine online blogger.

The decision of platform for professional bloggers is WordPress.org. Although you have to purchase your own domain hosting and name, the WordPress blogging software is free and there are many designs and features which you can use to suit your style and market.

Select A Niche

You intend to choose a well-defined niche. In case your market is very focused on a market you will be more focused on the kind of content you create as well to be able to monetize it easier.

Know Your Audience

You should be clear on who your audiences are precise. Who are they, which kind of job do they have, how much cash do they earn, what do they prefer to do in their leisure time? You ought to be able to know very well what gets their interest really.

Persistence Wins

You will need to update your site with fresh content to get the most traffic regularly. Writing is a skill that gets a complete lot easier and far better the greater you need to do it. If you get it done every full day, you'll create a process that automatically gets your creative juices flowing and indicators to the mind that it is time to create.

Generate Income From Your Own Blog

Once you get a good amount of quality content on your blog it is time to think about how exactly do you will generate an income. Begin to expose a few products to market and do not engulf your visitors with way too many adverts. An excellent mixture of affiliate products as well as your own products is effective generally.

Don't Quit

Generating money by using a blog is a long-term strategy. You should be willing to maintain it for the long-term. You will not take up a blog and make money immediately. Nevertheless, you can make money blogging, or earn more money at your business through blogging. Take into account that when to come quickly to writing blog posts, where which will, there's a means.

Today, anyone can begin a blog in a short while. Fundamentally, a blog is a highly effective marketing tool that will help you generate a great deal of money if done the proper way. However, if you would like to be proficient at it, know that you'll require to choose and walk on the right path. Given below are a few tips that you need to know to go on this adventure prior.

Effort And Time

First of all, be sure you know why you're going to start a blog. What's your purpose? Do you want to begin a blog to generate income online just? If this is exactly what you want out of your site, know that it will not be your path to take.

For making profits on the internet, blogging is one of the hardest methods. Associated with that writing blogs frequently takes a great deal of time and effort. It might cause disappointment if you publish something and nobody reads it. Immediate results should not be expected.

BLOGGING IS NOT FREE

Although you can choose Tumblr, Medium, Blogger, Word Press, Weebly, Wix to host your blog for free, know that you will have to lack control and lots of limitations.

If you need a customized web address, more storage, better design, and other features, you might opt for a self-hosted Word Press blog. The cost of a website and the hosting will be around $100 per yr, which is not a huge deal.

CHOOSE YOUR NICHE

Once you have decided to proceed, you may want to choose a niche first. What you ought to do is a choose that you will be thinking about. Aside from this, make sure that the one you are going to choose can help you stand yourself from the group as there are numerous blogs in each specific niche market.

One important thing that you must do when choosing a distinct segment is to define your audience first. Apart from this, you will need to think about your concerns, passions, and needs as well.

CONTENT IS KING

If you want to maintain or raise your traffic, know that the content is actually important. You don't have to publish tons of content every day. A couple of are enough, but make sure each post is high quality, this means it will offer something valuable to the visitors.

If the readers are able to solve a problem by reading your posts, know that they can bookmark your web pages and will get back again for more information.

KNOW BASIC SEO

When you have got the hang of basic SEO techniques, know that they can prove really effective in helping you get traffic for your blog. For growth, you need to get organic traffic for your web pages and SEO can help you do just that.

CONCLUSION

Nowadays, you could start your own blog within minutes. However, keep in mind that blogging might not work for everyone out there. Most newcomers leave this field in a few days or weeks. At first, it'll be harder to generate content but you will get used to it with time. So, you 'must' have patience and await your blog to create money and traffic.

Chapter 3. **Photography**

Would you like to sell your photos online and earn some cash? Questioning which websites allow you to sell stock photos?

Being a photographer, you can simply earn some extra cash (or even start a new career) if you know the right places to market your photos online. Photographers of various skill levels are in high demand because of their work, now more than ever. Everyone from large companies, medium and small size businesses to bloggers, graphic designers, marketers, and publishers buy and use photos online regularly.

The days of stealing images are becoming numbered due to tools that can certainly match pictures and their originators. For some legitimate firms, the lawsuit is not worthwhile. That's great news for photographers looking for continuing income while safeguarding their work.

Which kind of images are they purchasing the most of?

- All types of People – Kids, adults, various cultures.
- People working – Very popular with businesses. Folks working on laptops, writing, speaking at a meeting,
- Food – Various types of delicious foods even empty unwashed plates.
- Tools – Gears, hammers, nuts, bolts, and screws can convey a lot of things for potential buyers.
- Cities – Cityscapes, buildings, people commuting.
- Nature – This is a no-brainer which never gets old to shoot or sell.
- Travel – Shots from around the world are always in high demand.

Top 5 Places to Sell your Photos Online and Make Money,
1. Shutterstock
2. Fotolia (Adobe Foto Stock)
3. Alamy
4. Etsy)
5. 123rf

We discuss Shutterstock today. Shutterstock.com is a worldwide marketplace for selling high-quality photos and videos. Shutterstock established in 2003 and their Headquarters is situated in NY. So it's been more than a decade since they have been around in this business has customers all around the globe. They are operating in more than 150 countries and offer digital imagery licenses.

Their basic aim is to help digital buyers and contributors to connect with one another and make successful transactions. You will find two types of accounts on Shutterstock. One is Contributor and another one is the customer. Contributors share their digital mass media they have created and Customers buy it.

SO HOW EXACTLY DOES IT WORK

Since you want to learn how to sell Photos and Videos on Shutterstock to make money online so we are concentrating on the Contributor part. Now Shutterstock offers a great opportunity for individuals who create digital content that includes unique videos and photos.

So if you're good at Video or Photography editing and Publishing then this site can literally make you rich. They have obviously mentioned it on the website that you can immediately start to get thousands and an incredible number of visitors and begin earning money. All you have to do is create exceptional images and photos. There are three types of content that you can sell on Shutterstock. They are,

PHOTO SELLING:

You can sell plenty of photos on Shutterstock so long as they may be in JPG format and are at least 4.0 megapixels. That means you will need a higher quality camera for the probably.

VECTORS AND ILLUSTRATIONS:

You can create Vectors and illustrations and sell them on this site also. You are able to submit EPS format documents with a maximum size of 15 MB or JPG images with at least 4.0 megapixels.

VIDEOS:

You can create videos and sell them on this website also. However, the video size should be from 5 to 60 seconds. Forget about no less.

So basically you can generate in quantity of ways upon this great website depending on your skills. If you're bad at photography nevertheless, you can create stunning illustrations or vectors on Photoshop or other tools then you are in luck. If you're good at creating brief videos you can earn a great deal with Shutterstock then.

TYPES OF EARNINGS

Shutterstock offers lots of ways that you can earn money from your digital content. They are:

25-A-Day Downloads:

Customers have the option to subscribe on a regular monthly basis and they can download images over a period of 30 days. Each and every time you image gets downloaded you will receive 25 cents. Now this commission can increase up to 38 cents as you reach better milestones.

On Demand Downloads:

Subscribers can get an on-demand subscription which allows them to download and use images up to a year. Within this model, you will be getting $1.88 per download. It'll increase as you get more downloads and site visitors.

Enhanced Downloads:

Customers can get an Enhanced Downloads license which allows these to download images for commercial use. In this case, you will get $28 per download.

Referred Subscriptions:

You can even earn 20% commissions by referring more customers to Shutterstock.

HOW TO GET PAID

As discussed above, Shutterstock gives very good commissions on sales that are generated by any of the methods mentioned. You can get paid by three methods, PayPal, Skrill, and Bank Cheque. The minimum payout for Electronic payment is $35 while for Check is $300. So that it depends upon you how you need to get your payment. Payments are calculated on the 1st of every month and are paid after 14 days.

FINAL WORD

Whether you are a Photographer, an Illustrator or a Video editor this site can be a present for you. You will not only start making a good amount of money from your digital content but you will also get guests from around the globe to see and admire your photos and videos. So be creative and upload as many photos as possible but make sure there is no compromise on quality because you will need to build your reputation too.

CHAPTER 4. AFFILIATE MARKETING

WHAT IS AFFILIATE MARKETING?

Affiliate marketing is among the best ways to generate income on the internet. There are various affiliate programs available, offering a variety of products. Now you will need to determine how you market those products to your site's audience. Below are a few tips to assist in improving your affiliate marketing skills.

You should only promote affiliate products that add value to your site visitors' lives. Promoting poor products just to make instant money is one of the quickest ways to reduce trust with your readers. Once that trust is damaged it is impossible to regain. However, if you concentrate on providing value in the products you recommend, your visitors should come to trust your suggestions and will continue steadily to buy from you over and over.

Likewise as collecting commissions from the perspective of the salesperson, the more you sell (as the affiliate), the greater you receive a commission. The process surrounds this technique. Different programs might have different payment calculations, but the majorities are depending on the following,

• PPC or Pay per Click - Every visitor that an affiliate marketer can send is the same as a specific amount.

• PPL or Pay per business lead - The affiliate marketer is paid with each sign-up made through his / her efforts.

• PPS or Pay per sale - The affiliate marketer can get a commission rate from a certain percentage of each sale she or he makes.

If you're planning to generate income from online, then you can start generating traffic from the subscriber list that you have previously designed to your affiliate links. The total amount that an affiliate can get from affiliate marketing depends on the product or service that you will be selling. Some who could actually choose a great product can generate profits from sales they make and get their talk about of around 50 to 75%. Other people who can't find a great affiliate marketer program finish up earning a reasonably small amount because of the low percentage they can get from the commission rate.

Generally, the response to what is affiliate marketing is about promoting products as well as services online mainly. The way the process works focus on just how many people you can attract to go to a product's website or generate sales. If you are equipped with constant subscriber lists and also have an impressive selling skill, you'll be able to turn internet affiliate marketing as your basic income source online.

The Affiliate Marketing Business Model

If you're searching for a basic, proven business design for how to changeover from worker to the business owner then consider affiliate marketing. I believe of affiliate marketing as an act of writing one's own salary. However, the industry standard description is, The procedure for getting a commission rate by promoting others (or company's) products. All you need to do is find something you prefer, promote it to others, and earn a bit of the profit for every sale that you make.

The Process of Affiliate Product Sourcing

With tons of affiliate products and services out there and so many more coming into the marketplace every day, one needs a clear action plan to find a great product to promote. The 5 steps defined in the next section should get anyone quite close to their online business dream. The rest really depends on one's own desire to succeed online and a crazy intense interest in creating a lifestyle where you live, work and play by yourself terms. The only obstacle that could really be position in your way here is you the person and limiting beliefs we all seem to harbor within.

Five Steps on How to Start Affiliate Marketing For Beginners

1. Quality Is Key

Focus on settling for great quality products/services only. It's likely that whether its quality, the business's entire supply string process and customer care are of high quality too. It's also a good sign the company is founded on high integrity, has quality people as employees and is really out there trying to offer the best value in the niche market these are in.

2. A Big Solution For A Huge Problem

Look for niche marketplaces where there are big problems to be solved. Afterward, you follow that up with research for a quality solution. In a prior post on The Process of Affiliate Product Sourcing, I touched on why it is advisable to create an online business that focuses on fixing big problems and if possible, the very painful ones.

3. Look For Overwhelming Value

We live in a society where we are extremely informed and enlightened. Online responses and reviews can make or overnight break your website. Find a planned program that offers valuable freebies. The only reviews from your visitors, after they receive their free present, should be wow.

4. Integrated Suite Of Products

Accept programs which have a variety of other quality products that customers would want to keep returning for. Variety is good and it can help in creating a solid fan base also, which is wonderful for business growth.

5. It's All About You

Choose programs offering products that are an extension of you. See yourself using what you are providing, see yourself getting frustrating value from using that product, see yourself pain-free from the effects of the product.

Money Matters

Understand how you'll get paid. Read and understand the program's compensation plan. In the end, if you will work hard, re-skill and spend money and time on marketing, you should know the way the money flows back in return.

Research

As with any continuing business, do your own researches please remember the factors we discussed just. It's your business and nobody will brain your business much better than you. Think like a business owner and seek assistance from someone who's doing it. They could become your coach. Success leaves signs and walking in the shadows of anyone who has achieved the results you seek as an online marketer should be significantly considered. Getting started online is no instant success. There's work included.

The Guarantee Of Affiliate Marketing

Affiliate marketing offers a simple transition from worker to entrepreneur and with the right affiliate program, you could look cool carrying it out. Why? You might start earning and replacing your earnings prior to you quit your task and if this program is good, you could grab amazing marketing education and other business skills that will aid you well when you finally start your own suggestions to market.

Top Affiliate Companies In 2018

1. PeerFly
2. ShareASale
3. Wide Markets Ltd
4. Rakuten
5. CJ by conversant
6. Amazon Associates
7. Clickbank
8. Affiliate Partners Ltd
9. CrakRevenue
10. Commission Factory

Chapter 5. Sell Products On The Website

Smart entrepreneurs have recognized that more and more people are buying services and products online. The web offers of the very most profitable ways for business owners to reach optimum success and increase their important thing.

But how will you start offering products on the internet unless you have any products or services of yours?

Offering Products That Are In Popular

The trick to making reliable, repeatable money selling products on the internet is to sell something that is within high demand. You can sell any number of popular products as an affiliate.

This is actually the procedure for selling other's products and is recognized as affiliate marketing. You're called an affiliate marketer because you're linked to the individual or business that has generated that has created the product but you don't own any part of that business.

Right From The Start

Affiliate marketing is a popular and genuine online business model. The first place to start is with your interests and passions. How come this important? Well, generally, whatever you do running a business - be it an offline or an internet business - needs one essential ingredient. That component is your passion.

How Do You Find Products To Sell?

Among the great benefits of affiliate marketing is you do not need to buy any stock, offer with payment systems or arrange product delivery. The product owner manages of all of these issues.

Affiliate networks will be the best spot to find products to market. Registering for these affiliate networks is simple. Once registered, you will get products and services in about every niche you can think of just. You'll also have the ability to see which products are available the most and which products have the most affiliate marketers.

Some Of The More Popular Affiliate Networks Are:

1. Amazon Associates
2. ClickBank
3. PayDotCom
4. ShareASale
5. CJ Affiliate
6. JV Zoo

Check Out The Competition

Once you have chosen on your target audience and chosen the merchandise or services you are going to sell, take the time to check out the competition. What you can do to make your website more unique and participating? Why should people purchase from you instead of your competitors?

Selling Other People's Products On Your Website

You may sell other people's products as an affiliate without a website. But if you want to make the most out of affiliate marketing and earn more from selling products online, I would recommend which you have your own website.

Setting up a website isn't as difficult as you might think, and there are extensive user-friendly website platforms that can get you online quickly and easily.

CHAPTER 6. BUY A WEBSITE

Lakhs of websites are created every year, and thousands are either abandoned by their owners sometime afterward completely.

When you can buy websites with an acceptable amount of website traffic - and a demonstrated cash flow - maybe it's a perfect passive source of income.

Most websites use Google AdSense, which gives a monthly income stream depending on advertisements that Google places on the site. There may be affiliate programs generating additional income also.

Both income sources shall be yours once you get the Site. From a financial perspective, sites sell for 24 times their month to month income usually. So if the site generates $250 per month in income, you can likely buy it for only $6,000. Translation: a $6,000 investment will buy you $1,500 per the calendar year in cash flow.

You may be able to buy the site for under two years of cash flow if the website owner is especially anxious to get out. Some sites have good "evergreen" content that will continue generating revenue even years following the site has truly gone silent.

5 Important Tips Before Buying A Site

Legitimate forms of buying websites for a profit involve subtler types of portfolio construction typically, maintenance, and liquidation. Specifically, bloggers generally consider at least one of the next item before selecting investing in a blog:

1. The quantity of type-in traffic. If a blog name is brief, have.com as its top-level blog possesses searched keywords frequently, it could receive amounts of type-in traffic already. This can make your blog valuable to online marketers inherently, which explains why speculators utilize this as a criterion for selection often.

2. The number and quality of inbound links. Another criterion that bloggers use when selecting sites is the number of inbound links directing to them. This is an important factor in the secondary market (but not major market) for sites. In the supplementary market, sites were often hosted and promoted for some period of time before being sold; and, for this reason, often still have inbound links and traffic.

3. The top-level blog. A top-level blog is everything after the "." For instance, top-level websites include .com, .biz, .net, .info, .org, and a huge selection of different country codes. Not surprisingly, .com websites are typically more valuable than other top-level sites; however, short blog titles with country code or .info TLDs remain desirable.

4. A paid valuation. Many sites offer paid valuations of blog brands. Getting such a valuation is very similar to sending a piece of jewelry to a gemological laboratory to get a certified appraisal. It is important to note, however, that many appraisal services overestimate the value of sites. It is also important to remember

that the appraisal depends on market conditions; and will not remain true over time.

5. Whether or not the website is a "good fit" for an existing collection. Just as you would consider whether or not a stock is a good addition to your stock portfolio, you must make the same consideration when it comes to blogs. For example, if you're looking to reduce the risk of your portfolio, you might want to diversify and take on a larger amount of lower-value websites, rather than buying up a handful of expensive ones.

Of course, buying a site is a complicated practice; and these five items are just the starting point. However, if you begin to use these in your endeavors, they will provide an excellent means of avoiding embarrassing and costly pitfalls.

Chapter 7. Build An App

Mobile applications aren't only for large organizations; today many small or mid-sized companies own their individual mobile applications. The emerging trend of mobile technology requires more than simply possessing a mobile-friendly website. The combination of mobile application and business will be the best tool for marketing. In these days, you may interact with many small or mid-scale companies who own their dedicated mobile app. From the coffee shop to travel agencies, companies are gaining business through a mobile application and taking their marketing to next level.

Making Apps can be an incredibly lucrative income source. Think about how many people today have smartphones. It's likely that you're reading this on your smartphone. So people are downloading apps like crazy - and for good reason...

Apps make people's lives easier. Whether it's an app that helps people come up with nice pictures because of their blog or an application that keeps track of tasks, there are helpful applications out there for everyone.

You might be asking: If there are so many apps out there, why can you want to attempt to create an app? Isn't there a lot of competition?

Well, yes, but fresh, creative ideas can win. When you can come up with something unique, you may make quite a bit of money.

Simple - yet unique - applications can be pretty passive.

Don't know how to code? No problem. First, you can learn. Second, you can hire a programmer to build your app based on your idea. This could turn out being an expensive option, although it will probably yield a professional-looking app.

The end result is an application that has the potential to make you some relatively passive income. Don't downplay the idea to develop an app - it's a good one!

TOP 7 BENEFITS TO BUILD AN APP.

1. BE ALWAYS VISIBLE

Based on the statistics, the average person spends about two hours on a mobile device. As their use involves a handful of applications, it will influence just how they scroll or check the mobile for the applications they are looking for. By this way, the company can be benefited as the human brain unconsciously registers all the icons (with excellent design) it comes across - even if it is unnoticed.

2. DIRECT MARKETING

The mobile app provides common information about the business, prices, booking forms, features, user accounts, business news feeds and much more. The information that companies like to provide for the customers including sales special offers and latest announcements can be instantly added to the mobile app. You can certainly get closer to customers through press notification and remind them about products, special discounts, offers, and services.

3. Offer Value To The Clients

The company can provide direct rewards to the customers through the mobile application and it may result in more application download and more return customers.

4. Build Brand Awareness Among Customers

The mobile application is like a billboard you can certainly do what you want with it. The companies can make the mobile application functional for the customers. By adding attractive designs, functions, and options that customers love, the companies can build a superbly designed brand concentrated application. The greater you involve the clients in your application, the quicker they will buy your product or service and therefore, your brand will be popularized among customers.

5. Enhance Customer Engagement

Having messaging feature or chat will change what sorts of customers build relationships the application. The chat feature will get the work done within minutes without throwing away customer's time and also boosts business.

6. Stay Away From The Competitors

Possessing a unified design with interactive graphics and options will make an application stand out from your competitors. Be the first to provide mobile software for your customers.

7. BUILD CUSTOMER LOYALTY

As the companies approach consumers through various kinds of advertising, we might lose the impact of customers because of immense advertising. To grow the business, the customer has to build trust among the audience because of their service or product. The mobile program will take your business nearer to your visitors and bring all your business products in convenient with a simple mobile app.

Once you create an app, it can generate revenue for you while you sleep.

CHAPTER 8. DEVELOP A ONLINE COURSE

WHAT IS AN ONLINE COURSE?

An online internet course is a digital product that teaches students a skill or provides them with knowledge using digital media. Instead of visiting a physical class, students access the course content via the Internet. Online courses may also be referred to as distance learning or e-learning.

A lot of online courses feature text-only modules, while others incorporate video, audio, and graphic media to help engage students. By the end of an online course, the student should walk away with the knowledge he or she did not have before.

Do you need a special certification, license, or degree to generate an online course? Of course not. Today's educators don't always work for accredited colleges, and many of the finest educators sell online classes commercially to benefit from their hard-earned knowledge and skills.

Some online courses come from universities and schools, but anyone can create an internet learning tool and benefit from it. There are a variety of ways you can produce and sponsor your own online course. One very simple way is to use a website's like Teachable.com and Udemy.com.

WHAT DO YOU WANT TO TEACH?

Now that you understand you can online develop a course, what should you teach your students? Online teachers have created classes around a number of subjects.

Photography
Cooking
Fitness
Marketing
Sales
Graphic design
Beauty
Fashion
Leadership
Technology
Music
Personal development
Spirituality
Finance

This represents just a small sampling of topics that give themselves to online courses. In reality, you can train people how to do just about anything online. if you think about how you'll switch your knowledge into content. If you're not yet experienced creating a video, you might choose a topic that you can simply describe through text and photographs.

How Long Does It Take to Create My Online Course?

Some people spend weeks or even a few months putting together an in-depth course, while others can create a relatively simple course in simply a few days. Remember that everyone works at his or her own speed.

The length of time you depend on your course depends on several factors.

1. Length of the course
2. The complexity of the topic
3. Number of resources you need to make (e.g. video, images, graphics)
4. How you present the info

Even though you spend several months on an online course, the product becomes a source of passive income. In other words, however, you might revise the content from time to time, you never have to recreate the course, but you can continue to sell it to as many people as you want.

What Technical Skills Do I Need to Start a Course?

Depending on the type, of course, you decide to create, you need to know how to employ a digital camera, upload images to your computer, and edit image data files. The same goes for video and graphic elements. However, you don't need those skills to create a profitable course.

HOW TO CREATE AN ONLINE COURSE IN NINE EASY STEPS:

1. Choose a Platform for Your Online Course

2. Select a Course Topic and Direction

3. Look at Top-Performing Content

4. Find the Right Medium for Course Material

5. Create Content for YOUR WEB Course

6. Set Online Course Rates

7. Market Your Online Course

8. Measure, Evaluate and Adjust

9. Don't Be Afraid to Fail

Follow these steps and create an online course. Once you create an online course, it can generate revenue work for you while you sleep. Actually, you can create several packages at different prices. Some people will want everything, so you can include 'the works' for the highest price point and then have two lower price points to enable you to receive the largest possible volume of orders.

CHAPTER 9. WRITE AN EBOOK

This is often a lot of work upfront, but once the ebook is marketed and created it can offer you with a passive income stream for years.

You are able to either sell the ebook by on your own website or offer it as an affiliate arrangement with other websites offering content related to your ebook. After talking with several ebook authors, most of them inform that enough time spent placing these books jointly feels as though finding free money by the passive income they have today. Hardly any writers see any success off their first book, often it's their 4th or fifth that is sufficient.

Before you begin, it's worth considering the kind of book you want to create. Are you writing a fiction or nonfiction book? If it's a nonfiction book, what specific niche market are you writing for? Guides and tutorials work very well because people can study from them. If you're writing a fiction book, what genre are you concentrating on? Crime thrillers, illusion, romance, and chick-lit have a tendency to sell well. They are the overall types of ebooks that sell well, maybe because the followers of these kinds of books tend to read more than the common reader.

Consider the length of your ebook. Lots of the top-selling books have a tendency to be brief, quick reads that individuals can continue reading the commute to work.

Once you've written your book, be sure you proofread it for just about any mistakes. Maybe it's smart to pay a specialist editor to veterinarian your projects before you publish anything. There is certainly nothing worse than reading something with poor grammar and spelling! When you have paid for it especially!

STARTING AN EBOOK BUSINESS - WHERE YOU SELL?

As an ebook publisher, you have a few possibilities for selling your works.

You can create your own website and sell your ebook directly online. You may make a PDF open to your readers for example. A simple shopping PayPal or cart link and you're ready. A reader comes to visit your site, they order, plus they get a download hyperlink and get the book. It's virtually all automated, and you simply keep an optical eye on things to ensure the site is running smoothly.

The advantage of this is you control the whole process, get all the customer information (and that means you can promote additional products, services, or books), and you may charge higher prices.

Among the easiest ways to market ebooks is to sort out a third-party site like Amazon. You might have purchased products, books even, from Amazon before. But this is a completely different side to the massive e-commerce site.

The best benefit to working through Amazon Kindle Direct Publishing, though they ask you for a commission on your sales even, is their reach. Around 89 million People in America are said to be active ebook readers. That's your potential audience, those social people going to this website and searching for fresh books. Maybe it's your book they find when doing an explore a related keyword. Actually, 38 percent of daily sales of ebooks on Amazon go to self-published titles.

While you might not make as much money as you would selling directly on your own site, you should have the chance to reach an audience whom you wouldn't otherwise get access to.

The procedure of selling your ebook on Kindle is easy. You sign up and then upload your ebook. They care for converting it with their suitable format. Are you ready to sell and increase your business through Amazon?

Which of the options in the event did you go with? I would recommend doing both.

Put one (or two) of your books on Amazon and think of this as a traffic source... a genuine method for new visitors to find you, and you can make revenue from the sales of the ebook. Use your Amazon ebooks to drive a vehicle people back again to your website and have them on your email list.

Once you've them on your email list you can follow-up with them and sell them additional ebooks from your site, at an increased price point. Utilize the best of both global worlds!

WHERE YOU MIGHT GET YOUR CONTENT

Believe it or not, you might have the majority of an ebook written already. If you're earning money with a blog already, those blog posts could be converted into an ebook with some editing. Collect relevant blog posts into an order that makes sense simply, make any needed edits so that references that aren't relevant are applied for, and add a conclusion and introduction, and you're done. Any blogs you utilize should cover the same or related work and topics well together.

Obviously, that's only 1 way to construct this content for your ebook. If you wish to publish a genuine work of fiction or non-fiction - something you write yourself fresh - that is also a great option.

The main element part, if you're beginning with scratch, is to work at your targets of finishing that publication steadily. Write something every day! Start with an overview and fill up it in.

You can even repurpose a publication that is in the public domain. This means the copyright has expired and anybody can take the content of those books, and publish them, either up to date or reworked for some reason or as is. Did you observe that book, Satisfaction, and Prejudice, and Zombies that came out a few years back? That's a great example of reworking an open public domain book.

You'll find public domain works, which include classics like Call of the Wild by Jack London and Shakespeare and books on just about every subject you can think of (a quick search yielded dog training manuals, a how-to guide for amateur singers, and much more), in places like Project Gutenberg.

Another option is you can hire someone else to write a book for you. This is really a very common practice in the book publishing industry; these writers are known as "ghost writers".

A final thought to keep in mind is you do not have to create something like War and Peace. You are able to write shorter books for Amazon and sell them lower price points ranging from $2.99 to $4.99 and people prefer ebooks that are shorter with more focused niche topics.

How To Become a Professional Writer

You need to spend money to generate income, and this is as true with ebook publishing as it is with anything else. One important part of how to make money with ebooks includes investing in your job. Here are some of the services you might want to hire out which means you can make your book as professional and purchase-worthy as you can:

Cover Art.

Forget about seeking to doodle or freehand your own cover, and don't even think about just sticking a solid cover with an Arial title on your book. If you're not a musician or a photographer, find somebody who is to create a great cover for your ebook. Keep in mind, you only get one chance to make a good first impression, and that cover is going to be what your potential readers see first most of the time.

Proofreading And Editing.

Not all great authors are also great editors, and your digital grammar checker of choice isn't going to be enough to catch every possible error. Even if you are usually a perfect writer, it's almost guaranteed that someone else will be able to find awkward wording or places where you've used a wrong phrase.

Formatting Help

Depending on which platform you're using, there will be some distinctions in the formatting that you use. If you're computer-savvy and you also don't mind following a step-by-step instruction manual when it comes to formatting, then you could cut costs and do it yourself.

Marketing Your Ebook

Social Media.

Leverage your Facebook page, Twitter, LinkedIn contacts, and more to get the term out. When the book is published, post it on Facebook with a link back to your website with more information and way to order.

It's also advisable to promote your book on your blog, get active in forums related to the topic your book is about and tell people about it, and if you have a contact list, be sure to market it there too.

You might also provide a free chapter of your ebook. Which will get readers hooked so that they want more and will buy the rest of the ebook?

The key is usually to be proactive with your marketing efforts to continually generate buzz and interest for your book. Also, if you're selling your ebooks on Amazon you can certainly do paid advertisements directly on Amazon to market your books to a highly targeted audience based on keyword searches and specific products.

Other Ebook Selling Platforms

1. Nook
2. I Books
3. Smash Words
4. Kobo
5. Scribd

Chapter 10. Sell Your Own Products On The Internet

The options here are endless - you can sell about any product or service that you want just. It is actually a product you have created and can produce by yourself or maybe it's digital in characters such as software, DVD videos, or instructional videos even.

You can create your own website because of this goods and services until you have a website or blog set up already. Alternatively, you can sell it with an affiliate marketer basis also, either by offering it right to websites and websites related to your service or product or through a platform such as Click Bank.

In the event that you make big money in your present job and you're not sure that you may make an identical amount by selling products online, reconsider.

You can learn to sell products too and make quite a little money online. While it's not completely passive, it's certainly more passive than waking up and moving out the doorway to work every morning!

What Products Can You Sell Online?

I understand your first question raises in your thoughts is that what to sell online. You aren't finding what products is it possible to sell so those will provide you with a good profit margin online.

If you're still struggling with what things to sell online still, below are a few recommendations that will definitely help you to begin your first online business:

Books: Selling books online from your home is very simple on any eCommerce marketplaces. Amazon.com offers you a good chance to sell books on their platform in simple actions.

Niche products: Offering unique/ specific niche market products is the most profitable ways to do business online. These niches are available by you products from your local vendors.

High-demand products: Selling products that are bestsellers is one of the safest means of starting an online business. For this, you have to do some considerable research for finding best seller products in recent days. When you shall get a summary of best seller products, then you select which products are easily available to your location and those can provide you good sales and margin also.

Funky digital products: Some countries are hubs for production funky, quirky, and unique products at less price extremely. You can import these products and resale these at high prices easily. So, the customer's attention will be high for these products.

Products that aren't available offline: selling the product that's not common offline is a good idea to sell online first-time. You may already know that some products are extremely difficult to get offline. The manufacturers don't provide enough units to the offline retailers sometimes. So, the clients search the products online. When you have imported these products on your web store, automatically customers will proceed to your store then.

WHERE CAN YOU SELL THE PRODUCTS?

Yes, the merchandise has been arranged by you that you want to market online. However, the problem is where you can sell the products now. The answer is- online platforms.

Among the low risks, easy and quick ways to begin a continuing business is to sell products online from home. Here I've shown 2 big online places where you can sell products online from your home without any difficulty.

1. AMAZON:

Amazon is a Well known, a very big player of eCommerce industry, Amazon is typically the most popular among buyers and retailers. Founded by Jeff Bezos, Amazon.com is the world's largest internet company by income.

Amazon provides an offer to market your products on its system. You will need to join up yourself as a seller on Amazon.com.

2. EBAY:

When you have old items lying around your home, they could be sold by you for cash on the world's number 1 auction site eBay. The main benefits of selling on eBay include leveraging the website to operate a vehicle additional traffic to your website and can improve brand reputation.

You list something today, tomorrow you get customers. You don't need to get worried about promotion, discovery, and traffic. That's what eBay will best for your business.

CHAPTER 11. YOUTUBE

You can create videos in any area that you want - music, tutorials, views, comedy, and movie reviews - whatever you want, and put them up to YouTube.

After that, you can attach Google AdSense to the videos, which will overlay your videos with automated ads. When audiences simply click those ads, you shall make money using AdSense.

You must create compelling videos, to market those videos on social media websites, also to create enough of these that your earnings shall be via multiple sources.

You may want to learn something about video editing, but there are applications that can make that much easier and affordable these days. Still, there's a good little bit of work that switches into creating videos. But once a video is performed it may become a completely passive cashflow source for a long time.

The key to succeeding on YouTube is creating content and promoting it through another channels-your own site consistently, for example. Once YouTube notices that you're uploading new, quality content on a constant basis, it shall start showing your videos to people who are viewing similar videos. That's where in fact the advertisement money shall move in.

Use YouTube to get traffic to your website. If you've owned a website or blog which earns income, you will need traffic.

Many websites were hard-hit by Google's Panda, Hummingbird, and Penguin updates. If this happened to you, you're hurting. You should use YouTube never to only regain traffic but increase it also.

Get started doing the Creator Playbook. Once you're set up, consider repurposing some old content into videos, as well as creating new videos. Ensure that you connect to your own website in the first line of your video descriptions, so you can funnel your YouTube traffic to where it is wanted by you to go.

Create products and promote them on YouTube.

If you're creating your own products or wish to, YouTube offers unlimited ways that you should promote your products and make sales. Products you can create include ebooks, apps, artwork, and music.

Create your products, and add these to shopping cart software. Use YouTube to market them. Add an URL link of your product in your own video's description, so that viewers can buy the product.

Sell others' products as an affiliate marketer. Thousands of companies offer attractive deals to online marketers who promote their products, including huge companies, like eBay and Amazon, as well as smaller companies.

Additionally, there are extensive affiliate networks you can join. These systems include ClickBank, Fee Junction, and ShareASale.com. To generate income from YouTube as an affiliate marketer, review your affiliate products on video, or create "how to utilize this product" lessons. Don't forget to link to your products in your YouTube descriptions - make sure you're making use of your affiliate marketer web page link, or you won't get credit for sales.

CREATE A WEB TV SERIES.

Love telling stories? YouTube enables you to create your own Web TV shows.

A comedy can be created by your series, a play series, or your own chat show. Remember that YouTube limitations your show's duration to 15 minutes only. To longer videos upload, you'll need to boost your limit.

If you're a frustrated display screen or Television article writer, get a few friends together, and record your own Television shows. You never know. In the event that you get a lot of views, you might create a new career.

TEACH: SHARE YOUR KNOWLEDGE WITH TUTORIALS

Courses are huge on YouTube. In the event that you learn how to take action, you can show others, and generate income from your videos. Gaming, Beauty, and technology videos are popular.

TEST- MARKET YOUR PRODUCTS.

YouTube can be an amazing source for general market trends - you can soon discover whether you're brilliant, innovative idea may very well be profitable.

one example is if you've got a good idea for a product, but need financing, create some videos before a Kickstarter is created by you through an advertising campaign. The views and comments on your videos shall let you know whether your idea is viable in its present form. The YouTube audience can enable you to make it viable even, which means that your efforts to get financing are successful.

CROWD FUNDING

Crowd funding is now increasingly more common with the launch of Indiegogo and Kick starter. Maybe it's a great way to obtain money if you have a good idea for a mass media task on YouTube. But not only does it create your initial fund it also contributes to establishing income and audience for your project in the future.

SEEK SPONSORSHIP

Plenty of company provides sponsorship to YouTube channels for direct advertisements nowadays. A common source would be Audible from Amazon.com which sponsor knowledge-giving show such as Vsauce and Veritasium frequently. The great thing about any of it is that you can directly have the sponsored amount rather than splitting it with YouTube.

To get to a sponsorship you may want to work on a detailed proposal about the items it is possible to provide. Be sure you know well about your audience and the brand you are approaching.

It is important to check on your improvement regularly to be able to show if you remain on the right track in terms of finance.

Set goals for you to yourself for the measure. If you do not meet the goals. The current way for income might not be working for you, or that the quality of the videos is dropping. It might be a signal so that you can work on some noticeable changes.

BE CREATIVE

Quality content is the important thing to attract audiences always. Also to have high-quality content you can't ever be insufficient creativity.

The web is changing so fast a trend will come and go within a week. New ways that you can gain extra income could pop-up without you noticing.

So be creative with your use of resources. Always explore new ideas and ways for the creation and you'll have unexpected results.

CONCLUSION

Passive income could work for you, no matter if you have a huge amount of money to invest no right time for you to extra, or $0, sufficient leisure time, and a spark of ingenuity.

While they could take some fortitude and financing, to begin with, the moneymakers upon this list will continue steadily to get you money long after you've devoted the work.

So take a look at what you're dealing with: establish your financial goals and determine how enough time, effort, and money you're prepared to put into the venture.

Whether you decide to invest, buy a continuing business, outsource your own, or receive a commission for your day to day routine, you can succeed from passive income.

What exactly are you awaiting? Place the seeds today with one of the above ideas on the list.

CAN I ASK A FAVOUR?

If you enjoyed this book, found it useful or otherwise then I'd really appreciate it if you would post a short review on Amazon. I do read all the reviews personally so that I can continually write what people are wanting.

Thanks again for your support!

www.ingramcontent.com/pod-product-compliance
Lightning Source LLC
Chambersburg PA
CBHW030514220526
45464CB00006B/2791